LATE EMPIRE

LATE EMPIRE

DAVID WOJAHN

University of Pittsburgh Press
Pittsburgh • London

The publication of this book is supported by a grant from the Pennsylvania Council on the Arts.

Published by the University of Pittsburgh Press, Pittsburgh, Pa. 15260
Manufactured in the United States of America
Printed on acid-free paper

Library of Congress Cataloging-in-Publication Data
Wojahn, David 1953–.
    Late empire / David Wojahn.
       p.   cm. —(Pitt Poetry Series)
    ISBN 0-8229-3793-X (cl.).—ISBN 0-8229-5530-X (pbk.)
    I. Title.   II. Series.
   PS 3573.044L38 1994   94-11757
  811'.54—dc20   CIP

A CIP catalogue record for this book is available from the British Library.
Eurospan, London

The author and publisher wish to express their grateful acknowledgment to the following publications in which some of these poems first appeared: *Missouri Review* ("Late Empire"); *New England Review* ("Extinctions," "To the Reader"); and *Southern Review* ("Workmen Photographed Inside the Reactor").

"Elegy for Empire" and "Emanations" are reprinted from the *Chicago Review*.

"The First Six Seals," and "Videotape of Fighting Swans: Boston Public Gardens" are reprinted from *Poetry Northwest*.

"Hive Keepers" and "Wartime Photos of My Father" were first published in *The Gettysburg Review*, and are reprinted by permission of the editors.

"Homage to Richard Kapusinski," "Tribute and Ash," and "White Lanterns" first appeared in *Poetry*, copyrighted by the Modern Poetry Association, and are reprinted by permission of the editor of *Poetry*.

"Human Form" and "Tomis" are reprinted from *Triquarterly*.

"My Father's Pornography" is reprinted from the *Agni Review*.

"New Orleans, Unearthing" is reprinted from *Boulevard*.

"Photo of My Father in a Snowbound Train" is reprinted from *The New Criterion*.

"A Print of the Expulsion" is reprinted from *Crazyhorse*.

"Sorting the Personal Effects" is reprinted from the *American Voice*.

"Xerox of a Photograph of Bergen-Belsen" is reprinted from *Ploughshares*.

ANTHOLOGIES

"The First Six Seals" first appeared in *Pushcart Prize XVIII: Best of the Small Presses*.

"Human Form" appeared in *What Will Suffice: Contemporary American Poets on the Art of Poetry*.

"White Lanterns" appeared in *New American Poets of the Nineties*.

"Xerox of a Photograph of Bergen-Belsen" appeared in the *Fine Arts Work Center Anthology*.

Thanks is due to the Illinois Arts Council, the Corporation of Yaddo, the Poetry Society of America for its Celia Wagner Award, and *Poetry* for its George Kent Memorial Prize. Thanks also to Mark Doty, Jim Harms, Dave Jauss, and Dean Young for their generous reading and suggestions. And most grateful thanks to Lynda, "whose accent no farewell can know."

Book Design: Frank Lehner

Cover Painting and Section Dividers: Giovanni di Paolo, "The Creation of the World and the Explusion From Paradise"

In memory of my mother and father,
and to the memory of Lynda Hull, 1954–1994

What are words, I want to ask you, what
is clarity and why do words keep burning
a century later, though the earth
weighs so much.

—ADAM ZAGAJEWSKI

Oh phantoms.
Oh the many lives that have fountained through
My own. Soon, soon, I shall stop upon that platform

& you shall meet me there, the world rosegrey beyond
the scalloped tops of buildings & we shall seek
that thing which shines & does so much torment us.

—LKH

Contents

I

LATE EMPIRE

The hours, ripe apples, hang. The pleasure boats
        dapple the artificial lake, the women
                shadowed by silk parasols, hands caressing water,

the men in powdered wigs, half-dozing at
        the oars, and above the palace of Versailles
                the globe airostatique, tasseled and swollen,

a Fabergé egg, labors to the sky
        with its wicker basket cargo—a puzzled drake,
                a rooster, a goat dubbed *Climb-into-Heaven*—

the brays and crowing wavering above
        a hundred thousand pointing fingers, and the din
                giving way to collective gasp, the one breath

inhaled, exhaled, novitiates all; the halcyon
        days before the bells of sirens peal, blackout,
                a night sky riddled with searchlights. But here?

The Screaming Blue Messiahs erupt from the stage.
        Drums hiss at bass; the giant shaved-headed
                singer strikes a pose, a chord, hulking

maniacally into *The Wild Blue Yonder*
        amid a light show of dive-bombers—Stukas—careening
                ever downward, feedback ricocheting

the walls. London, the Town and Country Club,
        and I've lost you in a riot of green spiked hair,
                slam dance, combat boots, the crowd awaiting

the next upheaval, the storming of the palaces
of the ancien régime . . . *If I die in a combat zone*
box me up and ship me home. Footage

of fire, Dresden and its million pounds of napalm,
the singer clubbing his guitar to wire
and splinters on the stage, and I've lost you

to the noise and tidal dance floor. *I am*
the destroyer, I am the des-troy-er.
A skinhead waves a broken bottle at

a scared Bengali kid, and the light show
bends their flight to slow-mo; the kid leans down,
hugs himself while his friends crowd by, his sleeve

in bloody shreds. The room speaks the language
of last summer's recurring dream: the terrible
incinerating light has come, the dead

frozen black to the wheels of their cars, and I weave
a path among them to a house no longer standing,
call you in the way I call you now,

deaf to my own voice, and it's now
I see you lifted skyward by the crowd,
passed with half a dozen others on raised arms,

weightlessly buoyed to the music's stammer,
passed backward and forward across the dance floor,
a zigzag slither, until you finally come to rest,

earthbound again, on wobbly feet by a dull red
      EXIT sign, and I'm threading my way through the faces
            to reach you, shards of the guitar tossed snarling

to a sea of hands. . . . And when the balloon reaches
      three hundred feet, an early fall wind propels it
            beyond the lake, His Majesty's deer park,

the ersatz peasant village of the Queen,
      and when it blunders and falls to a field ten miles
            away, imagine the terror-struck farmers and milkmaids,

lamenting the fall of the moon. Before them the goat,
      no longer dazed, grazes on some clover;
            the broken-winged rooster staggers in circles.

Now fear has raised a hundred pitchforks and scythes.
      Now the fallen moon, and its cargo, must die.
            How can we blame them? They set the field on fire.

EXTINCTIONS

i

Dodos Hunted by Dutch Sailors: Mauritius, East Indies, 1623

Bodies almost globular, they can't
Be said to run or flee. They navigate
This field with dumb aplomb, fat men on a drunk,
Zigzag stagger, bobbing heads, destitute

Of fear or flight, their wings thalidomide
Stumps. A contemplative Captain Van Der Huss
Records it in his log—amble up beside
One slowly, wring its neck, the arquebus

Not even fired. By sundown his men rig pens
To herde them in like sheepe. But to execute
Them in such numbers takes all night. *The henne
Doeth cry much like a gosling, the cocke being mute.*

The fflesh, I must adde, is quyte tuff. By dawn
His men are splayed exhausted on the ground.

ii

*Passenger Pigeon Migration Observed by Audubon,
Illinois Territory, 1834*

Night sky at noon, the wings hammer air. Sudden ink
Of dark, the fluid eclipse, thunderclap stammer
Of the birds' push south. This flock, he estimates,
Spans two hundred and forty miles—over

Two billion birds. Shoot blindly in the air

And dozens fall. Twenty dead males spread out
Beside his tent, he stirs his watercolors.
Head, gunmetal blue. Neck, a murky violet.

Total length, seventeen inches: the female,
Of course, much smaller. Tonight raccoons will thieve
His specimens, overturn the rainwater-filled
Tin cup where his brushes soak. The 'coons will leave

His campsite in shambles, teakettle plunked in the fire,
His birds a carpet of purple feathers, threadbare.

iii

DOGS AT THE PAVLOV INSTITUTE: THE LENINGRAD AIR RAIDS,
SEPTEMBER, 1941

A hundred steel cages lined against
The laboratory walls. The sirens make
Them howl in unison, the whole beleaguered pack,
Each dog with a window carved into its chest.

Dr. Markov's taking notes, flashlight trained
On a collie bitch named Lara. Her pink heart
Beats a dizzy tattoo, her stomach contracts:
He sees them as if on a screen. He strokes her head.

Incendiary bombs ignite the Gorky barracks.
Markov's street goes up in flames. And Lara wails
For hours after the all-clear sounds. In March her tail
And paws will grace a soup, flavored with a leek

And the tongue of a dead man's shoe: Markov's last meal.
Then he'll lie down in snow beside the Summer Palace wall.

iv

Sunglasses: Air Raid Drill at Wildwood Elementary,
November 22, 1963

We snake in single file down the hall,
Child stars and starlets sporting shades,
To the basement lunchroom where we'll huddle,
Condemned to silence, ten minutes with our heads

Between our legs. *And if you sense a flash,*
I don't want you to look at it. Miss Bloom
Counts down the minutes, flicks the light switch
On and off. Then footsteps click across the room.

Whispers, and we file back upstairs
Without the films on hygiene or the wicked Reds.
Murmurs from every desk. Miss Bloom's in tears,
Her makeup streaks. Miss Bloom collects our shades.

Daylight presses in. The loudspeaker
Coughs on, the static bristling like gunfire.

CLAMOR

Climbing, tired, from the Green Line Station,
    she'd pass it on her way from work,
        the clinic where the demonstrators

waved signs—a doll in a noose,
    hung from a pole and spattered with red,
        photo blowups of fetuses, floating

ghostly as a star map's mythic swirls.
    Their mood was unpredictable,
        polite on one day, cursing on the next.

She couldn't tell why that afternoon
    was so different from the others.
        Hadn't she passed them each day for months?

And hadn't she come to know their faces,
    the same for weeks on end? But somehow a man
        was shrieking at her, was claiming that she

had just left the clinic. So now
    the crowd was chanting *killer,* and they danced
        around her shouting, one or two

even jostling her shoulders. Then she felt it
    graze her temple—a sharp, quick pain
        before the stone skipped across

the cobblestones beyond, a clamor
    high-pitched, distinct, even among
        the traffic noise and taunts. At home

she could just make out the bruise
in the bathroom mirror, the tiny gash
crescent-shaped against her temple.

Put it out of your head, she thought,
and from now on she would take
another route home. When she woke that night

and went to the kitchen to brew mint tea
she at first didn't notice the rain
merging with her profile in the window,

the clicks on the roof and eaves
as she bent toward her image,
violated now, like those women

she had read about in college, the watch dial
painters, heads bowed as they dipped
their brushes in the livid

irradiated paint, tongues licking brush points
for the detail work, the 6s and 8s,
the arrows of the second hands.

HIVE KEEPERS

In Brueghel's *Hive Keepers*, we watch as danger
twists their every movement into gestures

blundering and graceless, elaborately artless:
astronauts on Jupiter, divers

in a humming synesthetic ocean, the keepers
peer from crosshatched wicker helmets,

figures swaddled in fat cotton armor,
elephantine gloves wielding pine-pitch

torches, to trance the bees to sleep. And soon
ungainly slabs of honey will be pulsing

sunlit in their hands, the surgery complete.
How slowly such moments divide, multiply,

exhaust themselves, like the awkward silence
in the coffee shop, as Tadeusz attempts

to form the English words that name
the job he's doing now. *Azbesty*, he says

at last, *Azbesty*. All the way from Kraków
to peel asbestos, from West Side apartment

laundry rooms, from school cafeterias
in Harlem. Laughing, he tells me that at nine

twenty-five an hour he's rich, his bosses
important as Donald Trump, *Mafia men*

from Little Italy. He'll write back to Poland
he's a big-time mobster, so flush with dollars

he will buy a car, a microwave. The face
that stared puzzled in ESL—laboring

over *Why I Have Flown This Way to Freedom,*
and *Everyman in America Must Himself*

Become—all last spring for my pitying *C*
now radiates the confidence of smiles

in toothpaste ads. Like cosmonauts, he boasts,
they don their protective suits, spacewalk through

the basements to tear down each perilous
asbestos-mottled wall, though sometimes,

he admits, there aren't enough suits
to go around, and he spacewalks with only

a painter's mask, coming home with a cough, his hands
swollen pink with a rash that lingers for weeks.

And the others? Winos mostly. Often they'll
be sick on the job, muscatel for lunch.

And cancer? *Who knows, Sir Professor,*
about something you can never see? Always

He thanks the Virgin for his great good luck.
The moments divide, multiply.

He shows me his passbook, his Walkman,
photos of his fiancé in Lodz. And when

he's walked me to my subway stop, I watch him
saunter downtown, hands thrust in the pockets

of his Polish army greatcoat, stitch marks
on the shoulders where his corporal's stripes

were scissored off. He's gawking at the window
of a music store on Broadway, boom boxes,

guitars and keyboards, a legion of TVs,
tiered before a mirrored rear wall that hands

his longing back to him, red face swallowed
by the manic gadgetry, his fluttering palms

against the window like the trickster shapes
that dance from mirrors in Flemish paintings—

oxeye daisies and the grins of children
revealed, at last, as death's head moths.

New Orleans, Unearthing

No hammered golden mask of Agamemnon.
No fibula of Lucy in the Olduvai.
Only shame. Days of Nineteen Eighty-One.
No Byzantium. The shame won't die.
A Royal Street apartment looking down
On the Haitian bar. The necklaces of broken glass
Lovingly cemented to the windowsills. Eleven
Years older than I, she lived with me for less
Than two months. The bickering, the drunken
Nights: I had someone else by spring. But first
I helped her find the basement studio she took,
Its musty smell and flimsy backdoor lock. The rapist
Stabbed her sixteen times, a miracle she didn't die.
I was in Greece by then—my alibi.

My Father's Pornography

The semiotics not of sex but of concealment, the lessons,
    the legacy of dark.
It's a strongbox in the basement, a corner in his woodworking shop.
    Inside, a prostitute of
forty years ago is swallowing a massive, blue-veined cock.
    The man is wearing
boxer shorts around his knees, white socks. Another man,
    a black man, enters her

from behind. Her expression? Bogus pleasure, eyes
    histrionically wide.
The photographer, I suppose, is demanding she look horny.
    A few of the shots
are four-color glossy, most a grainy black and white. I've already
    said too much. What next?
The damp smell of the basement he so carefully paneled.
    No dialogue:

the father always silent as the men within these pages.
    How old is the boy when he finds them?
Twelve? Fifteen? Always the humid smell, his ears alert,
    waiting for the car-door slam,
the front door unlocking as his parents return from their
    Friday dinner out. Yes,
he is touching himself. The photographs. This is not how I meant
    to say it: start again.

In the bookstore, the shelves' collage of body and genital,
    stacked to the ceiling,
each book vacuum-sealed in plastic. From here across the room
    they're a sheaf of postage stamps
from some debt-plagued island dictatorship, its exports baseballs,
    wooden carvings, philatelic rarities,

And I am Baby Doc, my shades and leather coat, my kingdom
    Girls in Leather, American Erotica,

Hustler, Penthouse, Girls Who . . . The air
    conditioner, hissing.
Background music: big band songs. The curtained booths,
    my quarters. I would like it
to stop here. This should not be written down. Another poem.
    What could it contain?
A playlet. Empty stage and spotlight, my father lugging
    the strongbox from a corner.

Spotlight: my father in his hospital gown, the day before
    another week of electroshock.
If you look closely you will see him weeping, but I don't
    know how to tell you,
can't trust what I could say. I return to myself,
    and the curtained booth,
and the woman's face, crying too—the director no doubt
    goading her to grander

postures of orgasm, her blonde head thrashing, the film
    now wavering, flickering,
all the quarters gone. Then I'm paying for the magazines.
    On the car radio, white noise
of news and weather, Emperor Hirohito dying. He has not
    been told of his cancer.
Such knowledge, his doctors believe, will cause him
    too much fright. The Emperor has lost

a half-pint of blood, but today sipped a few spoonfuls of soup,
    his first solid food in weeks.

Homage to Ryszard Kapuściński

Aesthetics: San Miguel *Futbol* Stadium

Twenty thousand crowd into the gates—
Limon and tamales hawked from carts,

The mother, orbited by cameras, fidgets and waits
For her rebel son to die. The *Junta* must impart

Some lessons: let the people watch, let them dwell
On images.
            So Victoriano Gomez will be shot

By firing squad, on national TV. Martial
Music. Wind flings yellow helium balloons aloft.

Close-up to the face: Victoriano, shackled and flanked
By twenty riflemen, shuffles from the locker room,

Is bound against a pole. . . .
                A captain yanks
The limp head up. The boyish faces of his doom

Shoulder their American M-16s. *Make them watch and make*
Them think. Make them watch and make them think.

Aesthetics II: Addis Ababa, 1976

"When he had seated Himself, I would slide
The pillow beneath His feet. Our Venerable

Majesty, it is well known, had a stature quite small.
Yet the Emperor Menelik's thrones were high,

Poorly suited for His tiny son. The Lion
Of Judah's Legs—

               they could not *dangle* like a child's.

So I'd place my pillow with lightning speed,
Bowing as each Royal Audience began.

His pillow bearer thirty years!
                         Around the world
I went with Him, for protocol would demand

Each nation He'd visit to seat Him on a throne.
And for every throne I'd have a pillow made,

Its size and thickness measured exactly.
His Most Exalted Highness—

                    where could he go without me?"

Aesthetics III: Luanda Under Seige, 1975

Rebel forces have advanced to the outskirts.
Every night artillery fire,

               even dog meat rationed.

The theater owner's fled to Lisbon,
Deeding *Cine Mas* to his projectionist.

Just one film to show: *Emmanuelle*.
Over and over,

            eight shows a day, the house always full.

He freezes the film for the good parts. Catcalls,
contemplation.

          Heroic genitalia, eleven feet tall.

Start again, stop. Start again, stop. Klashnikov
and ack-ack fire. Emmanuelle and stranger on a plane.

Emmanuelle and several Kama Sutra limber men.
Start again, stop. Orgasmic finale. Grenade going off

down the block. Insult of multiple ironies:
The overturned jeep, the six dead Cuban mercenaries.

THE FUNERAL OF KHOMEINI, 1989

Can we blame the mob for seeking holy relics,
A fragment from the Mullah's robe, a handkerchief

Stained with His most precious blood? A copter must lift
The sainted coffin skyward:

                              the streets are too packed

For the hearses and the holy men to zigzag
Their path to the Saintly Tomb. The coffin's hooked,

A sea turtle, blundering toward air.

                              But the cables snap:
The turbaned body plummets like an oily rag

Doused with gas to set a house aflame.
Now begins the dark-robed conflagration,

Each chador a molecule, ravenous for oxygen,
Flaring white-hot. Now He is Theirs, and They are one

Devouring Alpha and Omega, each face a frame
In a film with a cast of billions. The future belongs to Them.

Terminus: Homage to Ryszard Kapuściński

Fissured with trash, a lot in central Warsaw: the film
Is running, a documentary for the BBC,

Lenses trained on Ryszard Kapuściński,
Who has witnessed twenty-seven revolutions.
                                                    We watch him

Point to the spot where the station stood, the terminus
Where the cattle cars were loaded for the camps

(Treblinka was closest). Gesturing, he is flanked
By a gutted sofa and two fifty-gallon drums, the detritus

Of what the glib would label *history*,
The moment's dialectic with the past.

But nothing is so easy.
                              Now he squints,
And points beyond where the station stood. *You see*

that tire beside the stump? There stood the house
where I was born. Only the past belongs to us.

Videotape of Fighting Swans, Boston Public Gardens

A white, reptilian, synesthetic hiss,
The frantic slither of reply. Sudden
Dart of yellow beaks: the necks entwine
Stumbling on the asphalt garden path,
Graceless as drunks below the necks, they waddle,
Trumpet, don't relent, not even when the cop
Dismounts to wrench the necks apart. Traffic stops
To watch, the trio lodged against a trash barrel.
Wild swans: but hardly those from Coole.
Not symbolist, not Freudian, just set to kill
Or be killed. So now it's the cop who takes control,
Unsheathing the rubber-tipped cudgel.
Nothing allegorical, just motion too quick to follow
And blow after blow after blow after blow.

Xerox of a Photograph of Bergen-Belsen

—For Henry Johnson

Thereafter, his lecture on graves. Yet these are not graves.
His lecture on well-organized hell. But this
is neither hell nor organized, even to form

discernible shapes. A handout: we reconstruct slowly,
roil of body on stacked body. And heads, oddly floating
to a surface, caught midscream and never

like Orpheus. The classroom's waxed-floor glare.
This ink and image, recollection of the camera's
remembering abstract eye. But not *eye,*

nor the echoing neural memory of eye, nor the memory
of the thumb of George A. Rogers, Magnum Photographers, Inc.,
pressing down the button to release the lens

to sixteen one-hundredths of a second's
glimpse of light. This room: midsummer sun
on rows of desks, the lake beyond and darkening sky.

Event and evasion, end link in the causal chain,
Already the linkage mere and neat. Mere and neat.
Bronze coins of the realm's most distant

satrapies, raised profiles of would-be Trajans or Alexanders
distorted to less than caricature. One hundred and fifty
thousand mummies from the valleys near Luxor—

human, cat, snake, and ibis—stacked on Nile docks
and loaded on clippers bound for Liverpool
and ground there for fertilizer, spices, aphrodisiacs

for Chinese coolies laying track in California
for the driving of the Golden Stake.
A warehouse of hair, a warehouse of shoes.

The Hotel Terminus, Lyon, a German military doctor
injecting Jean Moulin with methamphetamine
to wake him for his final beating,

personally administered by *Oberstrumfuhrer*
and former seminarian Klaus Barbie.
End link. The stifling room. The sister of Anne Frank.

End link. Limbs akimbo, patternless, water scrolls
in rain. End link, mere and neat.
A warehouse of scarves, of ladies' underthings. The window

blistering with rain, the big drops'
cough and hiss, and gazes
scarcely pausing on these shades, these pages.

Human Form

(Loyola Park)

Two weeks past Labor Day, the lifeguard towers pulled down,
replaced by Ukrainian crones on benches, chattering
beyond the yuppie jogging suit, scoring crack from a second

jogging suit, which nods. Blink eyes and the deal's done,
the black guy ambling off, the doctor/lawyer/investment banker
unlocking the door of his BMW. Mexican Independence Day,

raised banderas snapping beside braziers, women
in armchair circles, men kicking soccer balls, careful
not to spill their cans of Pabst. Local color:

that's the way to start. Voice off, long shot of the lake.
Caption: *Portrait of the Author circa Nineteen
Ninety-One (or two or three).* Time when the gods

descend to walk the evening, human form. May the author
now erase himself? He is tired of his small
mourning self. He has a working title: *Poem Without*

a Body Count. And yet. Did the gods descend to bring
his mother back in last night's dream, bald from the chemo,
raising herself from the car, one shoe off, that's all?

Close-up to the author, long shot of the lake, empty beach
but for this couple, operatically obese,
each of them headphoned to a metal detector, cumbersome

back and forth along the sand, like stitchery.
The woman gestures and the man grunts back. (May the author
now erase himself?) The woman bends down. This shape

she's taken, how slowly it sifts through the sand with a trowel.
Catch anything? Bottlecaps, quarters, someone's
cheap wedding ring, electroplated, gleaming. Yet this

is not a wedding ring but a coal, glowing as the woman—
believe me as I say this—places it upon
the author's tongue. For do the gods not have the power

to bestow such gifts of vision? And does the coal not burn me
even now as I speak? I am nine again and helping her
to stack the canned goods and radio batteries

in the basement fallout shelter, for Khrushchev is sending
missiles to Cuba, and if my father comes home,
tomorrow or next week, the room will be prepared

and we shall enter it as if we were whole,
a family. The coal searing orange, my tongue
composed of fire. My happiness as I hand her soup cans,

bags of rice. And from the flame I watch her hand reach out
to touch my hair, run fingers through it absently.
Of fire she has fashioned me, of sparks

flaring out with her strokes, cascading, acetylene white.

II

White Lanterns

i

Visiting Accounting, 1960

(The numbers hypnotize.)
Beside her desk, the three squat adding machines
Confetti the floor with paper strips in ever
Widening spirals, and her gaze dances to ledgers
Exhaling their breath of dust, a Dickens scene
Transplanted to the sixties, to General Tire
Or Northwest Bank.
                              (The columns hypnotize.)
                                        Released from Doctor Thorson,
My molar wrapped in tissue in my hand,
I peer into her office door. Lost in her lacemaker's
Trance,
          (The figures hypnotize.)
                    she sees numbers constellate into rows,

But not her son. Sixes and zeroes comet down
Relentlessly as sleet, the addition
And subtraction of these moments that compose
A life: this one to debit, this one to credit,
(She looks up.)
This one to crimson lipstick, vapor lights.

ii

Study, 1988

Her lipstick's crimson in the vapor light.
The funeral home basement, and the undertaker's bent
To pry the casket hinges up for us. No lambent
Painterly shadowplay, only stark fluorescent

Clarity. She's no one anymore.
Only the Christmas-and-New Year's dress
Tentlike on the wasted body, only a face
Half hers, half a cosmetician's caricature

Jerrybuilt from photos in a borrowed
Family album. Why must my mind so brokenly
Conjure this stranger's distracted study

Of wig and cheekbones, dental plates, of each bad
Polaroid of family dinners, summer cookouts,
His tools fixing the exact shape of her mouth?

iii

Harlequins, 1962

I remember the exact shape of her mouth,
The dime store novels on her lap, the lips
Working silent incantations, the threadbare couch.
She's in Rio tonight, or Pernambuco, and I'm up

Past midnight, creeping to the living room
To tell her I can't sleep. My father's on the road again,
The Fargo-Minot-Whitefish run, and I'm alone
with her all week, The Man of the House. Her gin

Glass sweating on the table, I watch her doze,
The book dropped to the floor. All night she's tangoed
With suave pencil-mustached generalissimos,

A rose in her teeth, absinthe and milky Pernod.
But now she's mine again, waking with a start:
David, fill the glass for me, I've got such a thirst.

MORPHINE, 1988

Johnny, fill the syringe for me. All the pain's come back.
Perhaps now she can sleep or watch TV,
Or stare at Midwest winter, snow shooting horizontally
From here to Hudson Bay. The flakes strike

The new picture window, and he fumbles with the syringe,
Waits through the game shows that she hates, until
She's gentled into sleep. And when she's still
He dozes too, fetal on the couch, the sponge

He dabbed her forehead with falling damp
From his hand to the floor. Refrigerator hum,
The clock spitting seconds, the seething storm,

The dog chasing rabbits in dream. Let them sleep,
Sleep as the spectral evening shadows come
To blur the window, the snowflakes' numb white lanterns.

V

WALKING TO SCHOOL, 1964

Blurring the window, the snowflakes' numb white lanterns.
She's brewed her coffee, in the bathroom sprays cologne
And sets her lipstick upright on the sink.
The door ajar, I glimpse the yellow slip,

The rose-colored birthmark on her shoulder.
Then she's dressed—the pillbox hat and ersatz fur,
And I'm dressed too, mummified in stocking cap
And scarves, and I walk her to the bus stop

Where she'll leave me for my own walk to school,
Where she'll board the bus that zigzags to St. Paul
As I watch her at the window, the paperback

Romance already open on her lap,
The bus laboring off into snow, her good-bye kiss
Still startling my cheek with lipstick trace.

vi

Picture Window, 1987

Spattering the room with a snowy trace
Of plaster dust, the carpenters have worked all week,
And the pane they're fitting will be huge, posed to frame
The brown November lawn. Thanksgiving break,

And we arrive to stacked lumber, sawhorses,
The living room a stage or excavation.
Wig askew, she slowly rises: the pain is worse
Since last month's visit. But she only complains

About the carpenters. "Two of them are *Negroes,*
And you know how they are. Your father has
To watch them all the time." The chemo's

Bleached her eyebrows to down, her voice a rasp
From radiation, red burn etching her throat and face.
Pineboards, hammers, sacks of nails. And now the stiff embrace.

vii

WRITING DESK, 1989

Frost-starred window, rented house, the stiff embrace
We share in photographs above my desk.
Mother and father, mother and son, faces
Sharing noses, cheekbones, our immeasurable strangeness

To each other. Perspective is a lie,
A blurred collage, and where does it carry us,
This trio waving from a thirty-year-old Chevy
Christmas morning, window starred with frost,

Colorless now, outside of history?
How would she tally fragments such as these?
I must be watching from the half-lit hallway

As she bends to the numbers. Neither of us speaks.
I move to the door, the churn of the adding machines
Fixing us here. The columns hypnotize.

III

WARTIME PHOTOS OF MY FATHER

i

Too far off, too faded: we do not see
The eyes beneath the helmet's shadow, cast
Like a veil against his face, angling vertically
To his arm, which clutches a Wehrmacht prisoner's epaulet.
A hangman's noose on the prisoner's neck. Caption:
Clowning around, near Rome, 1944.
I've brought the photo album to the lockup wing.
Electroshock, he says, has made a blur
Of all those years. No telling why he needs
Them back. The ambulance he drove. Palermo
And its DP camp. We sip stale coffee on his bed,
Flipping pages. *This man is someone I don't know,*
He says. A nurse brings coffee, his Thorazine.
This man, he says, *this man did not know shame.*

ii

M1 rifles slung on shoulders, backpacks
Spilling over, their climb up the hill to the blasted
Olive tree seems endless. When the German trips,
They kick him back up, the morning bracketed
With distant howitzer fire. A branch that's high
And strong enough is found. They drape the noose,
Abstractedly tighten it. One of *the guys*
At last, my awkward father makes a fist,
Snarling *schnell*. Now, predictably, the German's
Shit himself and mumbles prayers. But it's a *joke*—
They toss the noose to the ground. The August sun
Sharpens detail to a visionary glint
That memory can caress or kill. My father laughs
Along with them. The prisoner puffs a cigarette.

iii

And so the photograph. The prisoner's made
To smile, though shadows corrode his face, which grins
Like a skull, only mouth and chin revealed,
Disembodied, a jawbone picked from a ruin.
My father is connected to this shadow,
Angling to engulf his face. Does he flinch
Or laugh? Avert his eyes? Or does he smile
His buddies' regulation leer? The olive branches'
Shadows web the ground, complicate these mysteries
With intricate right-angled slashes,
Spoked against the sun's incendiary
Merciless bright. They'll snake their path
Back to camp, the German stumbling, head bowed
As his life comes back to him, a fever dream.

iv

My father, about whom I have lied. The photo:
Embellished for the sake of—what? A poem,
Though the hospital and war are true, the album.
But the German soldier, frightened to his marrow,
About to be hanged, mostly invention, an added
Dramatic touch to keep you reading on.
(*This man,* he says, *this man did not know shame.*)
My father, cruel to no one, cradled
In his silences, in a lime-green gown
By a window latticed with wire. But these
Unvarnished facts were not enough. I face
A man who weeps, his own face still unknown,
And I conjure his past for him. My shame:
Walking past the nurse's station, willing him someone else.

v

The secret missions of a railroad man, gone a week,
Then home a week, each morning sleeping in
To wake alone, his child gone and wife at work.
How did he pass his days? Imagination
Tricks or fails. Do I say he rose at twelve
To sausages and runny eggs? Do I say
He spent his mornings at his woodshop lathes
And saber saws, his wobbling carpentry
Filling basement and garage? *The Empire Builder*
Is an easier myth. Beneath Montana glaciers,
The engine straining, he leans from the baggage car door,
Surveying his domain, a scene I've written over
And over, into stupid wishful fantasy.
Now the real work: he blinks from mirrors at me.

vi

Look, he says, *I'm gone.* The mirror offers steam
Where his face had loomed. He's wrapped in a towel,
Singing Patsy Cline, lathered cheeks, a phantom.
Have we bathed together? And me, how old
Am I? Have I washed his back? No—I won't
Go on with this. Instead, the facts: he lumbers
Down the corridor from his shower. His roommate's
In a manic phase, and writing to some senator
About his *crooked civil servant son*—
How do you spell betrayal—E-L, or A-L?
I draw the curtains between the beds. Bathrobe open,
My father gives instructions for his burial:
Cremation, no headstone. Will I visit again
Tonight? Will I bring his spare teeth, a comb?

vii

Words to describe him: stranger, cipher, father.
The son invents a cruelty, a hurt
From years before the son was born—a unit
For measuring distance, the white noise that shimmers
Between our stuttering conversations,
Two men who cannot talk or touch. I wake
Alone in my father's house, and rise to pack
The things he's asked for, the widower's devoted son,
Wrapping dental plates in tissue, framed photographs
Of my mother, pairs of mismatched socks.
They've taken away his shoelaces and belts.
They'll search this bag I bring him, prohibit
Safety razors, sweets. They'll scour away his past.
Tabula rasa: the photo album shuts.

viii

MILITARY PORTRAIT OF MY FATHER
    (AFTER RILKE)

The eyes don't dream, though surely the brow feels
Something remote. Shut lips. Can we penetrate
Such reticence, this sorrow that admits no smile,
Only shadow? On the lap, his medic's helmet,
Scarred and pitted, white oval for the scarlet cross,
Washed-out colors, fingers toying with the strap.
The wrists, which won't stay folded for the pose,
Are milk white blurs, as if only the hands could grasp
The details of such inwardness. This time, no caption.
And the ringless hands, open or clenched?
Hands and eyes averted, the image beckons,
Then pushes us away. It haunts my desk.
I stare at the glass, my breath against his face. I stare
Until our images dissolve—*shadow into light, son into father.*

IV

PHOTO OF MY FATHER IN A SNOWBOUND TRAIN

Now that his name has turned to elegy,
The drifts compose their inexact refrain

As they did in Minnesota every January,
Less a music than a bone white flurry

Of notes calling forth this slide show in my brain,
Where I watch his face turn to elegy,

Then turn away. The snow will drift and bury
Memory and every patch of ground. The Great Northern

Stalled en route to Winnipeg, a January
Blizzard, '61. And here my father stays,

Long pulls from a bourbon flask, alone inside the engine.
The Empire Builder: its very name an elegy

To eras of diesel and steam. No clarity
To the slide: glint of the flask, a drift-bound train,

Gray light of Minnesota January.
Erasure, erasure, visibility

Collapsed to zero. Just an arm now, lifting bourbon
To the disembodied mouth, this elegy

That was his name, blurring to infinity,
Lost in the blizzard's relentless implosions,

Lost to this Minnesota January,
Where his name has turned to snow, to elegy.

TOMIS

Twenty miles south of Gary, and Chicago Spanish stations
  die, fields half-lit
at 6 A.M. So Tito Puente slurs to white noise-static,
  transformed to hog futures,
a talk show doctor of forensics droning on about plane crash data—
  "half the bodies

are mislabeled, for even dental records lie. Insurance fraud
  is money too . . ."
Speedometer at eighty, eighty-five, Elena's weekly drive
  to Tomis, Indiana.
Spanish for grades 10–12, ninety-five miles one way
  to the Loop, and six

thousand more to Buenos Aires, where spring's begun, her mother
  planting squash in the backyard
garden plot. At Tomis, Ovid ate red seaweed all one winter,
  and took years to learn
the native's guttural tongue. His pleas to Caesar, in elegant
  hexameters,

went unanswered. And these acned faces, Elena thinks,
  with their *Guns n' Roses*
T-shirts, and their twenty different names for getting loaded
  on Friday nights,
must be her version of Ovid's bearded, squirrel-eating
  Scythians.

Conjugate the verb *vivir*, the verb *llamar. Hola muchachos*
  y muchachas
¿que tal? Ovid died still begging for permission to go back.
  Elena has her green card
and refuses to return, for the past is fragments, itself a kind
  of exile.

Her mother keeps her sister's room exactly as it was,
        the walls a shrine
of photographs: Estella in the opera chorus, her first
        communion;
obligatory yearbook shot. And, atop the bookshelf with
        its volumes of Camus

and Marx, what must have been her final photo—grinning at
        the rally with her
college friends, one hand raised in a fist, in the other a small
        black flag. There's nothing
dramatic to tell. One night she disappeared. No ink-dark
        Mercedes idling at

her mother's door, no scowling men in trench coats jostling her
        away. No TV
footage of a hundred demonstrators handcuffed, clubbed,
        and brought before
some drunken civil magistrate, camera lenses flitting
        from face to face.

Only the call that afternoon that she'd be late, and the days
        of waiting arcing
into years, her mother at her vigil in the Plaza de Mayo,
        the *desaparecido*
madres circling the square, the children's blownup grinning faces
        almost solemn

on the placards, almost abstract. *The past is fragments.*
        Conjugate the verb
morir. Conjugate the verb *esperar,* to hope—the new regime,
        its promises.
And now see what they mean. The years of waiting ending with
        the phone call, Elena

and her mother in the waiting room, the city morgue at Cordoba
    where the acres
of mass graves were found, Estella's dental records
    in a file the doctor
rifles as he ushers them into the chilly basement room.
    Is it here the exile

starts or ends? Florescent lights, the verb *llamar,* the verb
    morir, the glittering
bones, the skull. "Your sister's left arm, was it ever broken?"
    Latinate barrage:
he scribbles on his pad. *Supraorbital Foraman,*
    Occipital

and *Temporal.* "You see here where the bullet exited."—
    He makes a red circle
with a highlight pen. Is it here the exile starts or ends? Skull
    and twenty-seven
bone fragments. They could fit in a shoebox, a hatbox, a larger purse.
    The doctor nods,

shuts the folder, caps his pen. "If you'd like I could leave you
    alone here for a while."

EMANATIONS

*"The God whom Schreber constructed was quite
peculiar, as limited in his way as an exigent and most
imperfect human being."—Peter Gay, FREUD*

Stalled here, bone machine in the peopled
    Sinai, he leans against the iron gate—*mother*
        fucker, mother fucker, and then the cries,

which blend with street noise, here at the study window.
    Stalled train, then commanded forward, lurching
        the alley in reply to voices' hiss

and whirr. The mind's overlit stunned trading floor,
    selling francs and buying deutschmarks, strips
        of paper littering the tile. We have tried

to talk with him, something about waves,
    emanations, the classic roll call.
        Soul murder. Like Judge Schreber in the Leipzig

asylum, the "so-called Devil's Kitchen,"
    the rays tormenting him. Evil's transmigration,
        against which the one below claps hands,

to protect himself. Expulsion from the Holy Land,
    which means a torn nylon running suit,
        the park at night. He recognizes L.,

who gives him a roll, orange juice. The Flight
    into Egypt-of-Perpetual-Voices, the mesmerist
        choir, which subsides when he's grown too tired.

And has left us tonight to the Starship Enterprise,
    to time-traveling aliens who steal the souls
        of cholera victims, turn of the century

San Francisco. Has left us to this photo
of my father, smiling from a dock in Minnesota,
no fragrance yet of unguents

slapped on his temple to assist
the conductivity of the shocks. A speech
by Data, the Android Candide:

*the Enterprise's mission . . . . to prevent them from changing
the entire history of the world.* Soul murder
unpunished. For seven years, from Italy,

North Africa, the milk run in Duluth,
my father mailed his father every paycheck,
to deposit in a bank account, this for

an education beyond eighth grade. And my grandfather
spent it all, on what I was never told,
though drink is the most obvious explanation.

*How often did the beatings occur? How many
years did they continue?* The doctor
in her sari asking if my father *often*

wet the bed. The red dot on her forehead,
the signing of the waiver forms. How light
travels centuries to halo the face, to dilate

the third eye, so open that it's blinded.
My grandfather rising from some feather bed, the belt
pulled tight between his hands. Triplicate forms,

witnessed and notarized. Judge Schreber believing
himself the last man left on earth, the doctors
and orderlies malevolent phantoms,

"improvised-fleeting-men," believing God
        was impregnating him, transmitting "the so-called
            rays of voluptuousness," to start the human

race again, to give the race its GI Bill,
        high school equivalency certificate.
            My father with his Bible, moving his lips

over Deuteronomy, practicing at night
        the Palmer Method, yellowed pages of *G*'s
            and *J*'s, to discover when I sell the house,

to think of when the Android's head, having lain
        on a mineshaft floor five hundred years
            is reattached. First the *L*'s and *K*'s,

then whole words, page upon page. The quick
        brown fox. The lights in the android's cranium
            begin to blink. The child Schreber photographed

in his father's invention—a patented device
        to improve the posture, into which the subject
            is strapped. A metal band for the head,

it resembles an electric chair, leather strap
        for the head, with a little give, so chewing
            and speech are still possible. The father,

in fact, is lifting a fork to the child's mouth.
        The quick brown fox. The head blinks on,
        blinks off. The attendants smear the unguents.

Apollo finds the kill switch for the crooning head.
        Endearments. The father in his morning coat,
            and the fork raised again to the child's mouth.

Elegy for Empire

i

The Journals of Aspley Cherry-Garrand, 1911

A six-week journey in Antarctic winter
In search of penguin eggs, and a canvas sack

Of lignite specimens, the cloth gone stiff
As sheet metal.
                        No feeling in the toes and fingers

Since 6/28 . . . Gums of Bill and Birdie
Seeping blood, discolored to licorice black—

An hour to chew their biscuit. Scurvy, I suspect.
Then The Grail:
                        the Emperors' rookery

Bustling as Victoria Station, at least
Six hundred in the midday twilight, guano

Piled like cairns, higher than the drifted snow.
As we approached, there arose quite a ruckus from the beasts.

But victory was ours.
                        To thieve the eggs was simple
And I pickled them in brine inside the igloo.

ii

The evolution of the flightless bird
Is, I am told, an enigma, hotly

Mooted in the realms of ornithology,
And thus my emperors' embryos
                              were offered

To His Majesty's Museum of Natural
History, South Kensington, and I thus

Received from Chief Custodian Mr. Burrus
A receipt for same
                    (tax deductible).

But it happened that some time later I had cause
To visit the museum with Captain Scott's

Younger sister Margery, who was wont
To view the eggs which had caused three men to risk

Their lives.
            They had, however, been discarded
years before: an oversight, I was assured.

iii

ICEMEN OF THE FRANKLIN VOYAGE: EXHUMATION AND AUTOPSY
OF HER MAJESTY'S SEAMAN JOHN HARTNELL, BEECHY ISLAND,
NORTHWEST TERRITORY, 1984

Hot water slowly pumped into the grave
and ice-bound casket
                will melt the permafrost

where he's lain wedged 140 years.
A deep red aura rims the skull—the handkerchief

his head's encased in, pirate style. Then eyes,
one gone milky,
                one still gunmetal blue.

The handkerchief floats up, releasing a halo
of fluttering hair, dark brown. Nothing in the good eye's gaze,

no ice-floe mazes from *The Terror's* mast,
no midnight suns of some
                chimeric Northwest Passage.

TB and emphysema, lead in lethal dosage
from the solder in his tainted food tins cast

him here, first to die.
                Pump-whirr and the hose's drip.
The Lazarus fingers quiver as the hands unclasp.

A Print of the Expulsion

This wheel turns the world: the firmament
is various purples, reds and blues, the raiment

of God the Father also blue. Angels,
naked, bird-winged, hover with swords of flame.

Beneath this painting Mother wept. Mother was
possessed by spirits who died in ancient Greece,

in battle, their names a clumsy Homeric pastiche
of ones she'd gleaned from children's picture books.

In trance her eyes would flutter, close, a cry
would build from far beyond—or so she'd say—

until Mentorius, or Masticus, or Ajax
Metaphorus spoke their guttural pep talks

and Mother's followers would nod, and fill
a wicker basket with large checks. She'd fall

to her knees, writhe and twist her head, shriek
but never mess her hair—a Holy Roller but discreet

and cunning. No, at first she'd rarely punish us. . . .

❈

The print: larger than life, anonymous

Sienese, c. 1520, so its cracks, miniscule
on a gallery wall, seem to web and fill

and shadow every angel, the palms and olive trees
set small within Eden's gates. Gold filigree

haloes an angel's avenging head, haloes
the distant throne of God. I do not know

how much or little mother believed, but when the church
grew too large for disciples' living rooms, a ranch

was purchased outside Butte. Mrs. Masterman,
renamed by Mother *Ampuna*—"Anointed One"—

for the most part raised my sister and me.
Mother, for the most part, raised funds. You see,

The End was coming, as it always must for sects
like ours. Like Origen, she hated sex,

apostasy, and Jews. Disciples paged
The Protocols of the Elders of Zion, tracts

from groups with *Aryan* in their names. And yet
our father was a Jew, and sometimes his lawyers would attempt

to win me and my sister back. By then
we'd all moved to the ranch. Mrs. Masterman

taught us martial arts, how to fire and clean an AK-
47 blindfolded, to give nothing but name and rank

to captors, then bite down hard on our hidden
cyanide pills. I was twelve, Mary eleven.

Mother took to channeling from a throne,
"transmitting" JFK and Charlemagne,

Savonarola, Albert Schweitzer, all of them
forecasting rains of fire, pronouncing doom.

Bodyguards barred our way to her. The print
got tacked to the fallout shelter wall. Only saints

of our church and beings from UFOs would survive
the coming conflagration. At five

each afternoon came drills that sent us down
to the bunker where we'd wait out Armageddon.

        ✪

Mary was fifteen by now, and met a boy.
Of course the news got back to Mother, for her spies

were everywhere. And for the first time in years
we were summoned alone to Mother's chambers,

Mary weeping, while Mother screamed the ersatz
Bible lingo she'd come to favor—*harlot,*

Whore of Babylon, and so forth. *This child
of thine, and thou as well, shall dwell outside*

The Tribe. Anachronism though: Mother beat her
with a rubber hose. And though they cried together,

embracing like real mother, real daughter,
it was only for a moment. Next day Father's lawyers

came to take her from the ranch. I lasted
another year, then left too. Mother'd prophesied

the exact date of The End by then. *By going with
those unclean Jews,* she said, *thou too shall perish*

in the fire. When The Last Days came she gathered
twenty in the bunker. With three weeks' food they sealed

the doors, and what happened next is speculation,
no diaries like Scott's, no tapes like Jonestown,

and I don't imagine mother's voices reached
any particular eloquence near the end:

Ajax Metaphorus screeching they bite down
on the cyanide they'd hoarded for years. The children,

I suppose, were first, kissed on the foreheads and warned
to ignore the bitter taste. And Mother, enthroned,

and I hope shaken out of her trance, by rights
would be the last to die. An arm outstretched, she lifts

the capsule to her lips, a litter of bodies
on the dais, like the ends of Jacobean plays.

It made headlines for a week, the network news.
Father's lawyers made some statements to the press.

At twenty-five, I inherited the ranch,
six hundred gravel acres that no buyer wants.

The buildings all were razed, though Mary keeps
a cabin where we stay a few weeks

every summer. I don't know how the print
got there, faded, God's blue robes washed out

to a feckless gray. The wheel that turns the world
spins colorless circles on a center mottled

and pitted as old photographs. Last August,
walking near the trash heap that was piled

by state troopers and federal agents
cleaning the Chosen's belongings out,

scavenging for clues to all that baffled them,
I found the canister—eight millimeter film,

frames of Mary, Father when he lived at home,
Mother in a dress, an ordinary dress, like anyone's

from 1960, pearls instead of diadems.
I'm five and clinging to her dress hem,

holding tight for hundreds of blue gray frames
as she steps from a car with massive fins.

I held us both this way, squinting in the midday sun.
But let the earth compose our change. I threw it down.

To the Reader

—Ruined Commune, Green Mountains

Sure, the Day-Glo driveway sign screams Dreamer's Road,
But no immaculate Shaker barns, no ark-
Shaped houses built without a nail: the geodesic
Dome's collapsed, and the shack where dope was dried
Before they'd truck it down to Burlington,
Each key haloed in recycled paper,
The leaves made potent with designer manure,
Wheelbarrowed up the south face of the mountain;
And Star and Peacepipe, twenty now, subliterate,
Pump Exxon Super in West Montgomery,
Disguised as name patches *Bob* and *Smitty,*
Though *Bob's* trailer wall flares Jimi Hendrix
Torching his guitar at Monterey.
Gentle reader: fuck you and your irony.

SORTING THE PERSONAL EFFECTS

i

The single letter she'd ever write him, March
Of '41. Would he come with her *to church*
And dinner Sunday next? Her tourist saltbox bed
Is *grand and firm . . . Saw* Citizen Kane. *It starred*

Joseph Cotton. Pardon my French—a load of crap.
Outside, Tallahassee palm leaves snap
In gulf breeze like an orchestra of trapdoors.
The requisite smells: orange blossom, oleander.

She wouldn't, of course, see Florida again.
Palmer method flourishes in every line,
Fluttering Gs and Ys, perfect oval As.
Fetish in a cedar box, a decades' long cliche,

Folded and unfolded. The creases tear.
The night here's . . . never still. White curtain, salt air.

ii

Nothing I'll remember or invent. Photographs
Of dogs, a legacy of Melmac cups,
Closets full of merciless knickknacks
Not even dignified as kitsch. Syrup

Bottles shaped like Butterfly McQueen.
Bronze Star, Silver Star, Good Conduct,
Discharge papers in a Woolworth's frame.
Harlequins, seven hundred: *The Paradox*

Of Rose Marie, Alhambra Lemon Blossoms.
Fourteen electric razors and his cache of porn
Concealed in the dresser by his cardigans
And lariat ties. What to save and what to burn?

An inventory, not a reckoning:
Kane's dropped globe of snow, still careening.

The First Six Seals

"I saw a scroll. It had writing on both sides and was sealed with seven seals."—Revelation 5:1

Seal I
The Three Christs of Ypsilanti

All three Christs in a locked room for a year—sharing meals,
A daily "business meeting," conducted, of course,
To *Robert's Rules of Order*. Each session commences
With a different song: *Blue Moon, Yankee Doodle.*
Never hymns, for they spark untherapeutic
Theological debates, which leave each Christ
Exhausted. Tonight they talk back to a TV set
Bolted to the wall. Joseph screams Leon's "a her-e-tic"
Who'll burn for watching *Sea Hunt, Milton Berle.*
Leon Almighty, Clyde Christus Est, Joseph Hallowed-
Be-Thy-Name. Pre-thorazine and manic, their godhead
Is degenerative. The experiment will fail.
For what could shame them into human form? Joseph bewails
Another lost *Yahtzee* game; Leon, scowling, changes channels.

Seal II
The Prophecy

"Then Mrs. Clark received the final message,
Spoken to us from her trance: prepare for the saucer
To land at midnight by the patio. December
In Wisconsin, it had snowed all day. She urged
Us to stay calm, to remove all metal objects
From our pockets and clothes, for in the spacecraft's heat
They'd scorch our skin. We threw down earrings, belts
And coins, sliced the zippers from our pants

And skirts. We gathered in a circle in the yard
And waited for The Mother Ship's approach
On this the final day of the world. Someone spoke
Of *this* snow as the world's last. Mrs. Clark
Led us all in *Amazing Grace*. Then the silence settled in,
The snow swirling up. We huddled that way 'til dawn."

SEAL III
SEMIOTICS, POSTERITY

"These fifty-gallon drums," he's telling me,
"Their water's radioactive two millenniums. . . ."
It's breakfast at the artist's colony.
His paint-flecked sleeve is reaching for the ham.
His grant's not NEA, but AEC—
Devise a "semiotic," a symbol still readable
In A.D. 4000, some ideogram for *deadly*.
"They'll stencil it in red on every barrel
They store. I'm working for posterity."
His studio's a cactus forest: six-foot exclamation points.
Thunderbolts and skulls like teetering stacks of heavy
Metal album covers. *"Hardest to paint
Are the simple things,* Cézanne said that, or someone
Like him. Just call me the goddamn toxic Cézanne."

SEAL IV
*THE ECCLESIASTICAL COMMISSION TO INVESTIGATE THE RECEIPT
OF THE STIGMATA BY MARY VAN HOOF, MARQUETTE UNIV.
HOSPITAL, 1952*

Holy Week in a psych ward cell—her hands
And feet are bandaged, and she claims to feel

The scrape of thorns all night against her forehead.
The stenographer charts each ecstacy, and all
Sharp objects have been taken from her room.
Blood tests daily: stigmatic blood in theory should be iron-
poor, its salt content low. Father Gray performs
His daily interrogatory. *How often does the Virgin*
Come to you? Is she, for example, right here
Before you in the room? What prophecies
Has she uttered in recent weeks? Is it true your father
Makes you sleep tied to a chair? Your mother—is she
Often hurt by him? Is it true he broke her collar-
Bone? What sort of hair shirt did he make you wear?

SEAL V

CATHEDRAL BUILDING: A PHOTO OF CHERNOBYL

Inside the reactor core, a zigzag pulse
Of light drilling through the wall's six-story crack.
The lead-robed worker turns to us, the camera flash
Reflected in his goggles, white-hot asterisks,
Exploding spiral galaxies. He'll die
Of thyroid cancer in a year or two,
But the work will last "at least a century."
Slow retrieval of deadly debris, the crews
Stabbing trash in Dantescan gloom, like artisans
In an antimatter Salisbury or Chartres.
They'll wreathe their labor in a concrete dome that's seven
Miles across, mausoleum of shattered atoms.
The lead-robed worker turns from us, descends
A stair. The camera hisses as the film rewinds.

SEAL VI
AFTER THE FUNERAL

Inside the Bible on his bedside table
An address decades gone: *ALBEE, S. D.,*
And *PROPERTY RC Wojahn P.F.C.*
The *12 Steps* of A.A.: "Expect a Miracle,"
Embossed in Gothic lettering. The 0_2 tanks
And tubes, a Kleenex box, his watches.
Bookmark at *Revelation,* verses scored with *X*es.
Now the trumpet blast. Now the lamb breaks
The Seventh Seal. And now The Wormwood Star,
"Like unto a torch," comes thundering from the sky
Beside his marginalia: "prophecy"—
With triple exclamation points. *Father,*
Where art thou as I call? Upon what journey
Did thee embark, that such signs could point thy way?

TRIBUTE AND ASH

i

A Landscape by Grant Wood

By an open barn door two cows loll,
A Holstein and a Guernsey, and a white
Horse grazes in the shadows of a hill.

A one-lane bridge, and to its right
A gravel road that winds some feeble
Mashed potato mounds—a Midwest

Effort at terrain, where barns
Outnumber houses, and a bone white church spire
Nudges the left hand frame. Not a *town*,

Not even a hamlet. Grain elevator,
Tavern on the riverbank,
The trio of rickety windmills, water tower,

Willows and some mystery trees that flank
The water, resembling puffballs or grapes.
Each night she'd come home from Northwest Bank,

From her ledgers and adding machine tapes
Littering the floor like barbershop hair.
And under these drab cornfields she'd smoke

The packs of Salem straights, curlers
Shaping their weird corona, romance
Novels and a highball tumbler

Replenished each hour with a splash
Of gin. The endless curlicues
Of smoke. For thirty years she'd cough,

Flip the pages while the white frame grew
The color of a spoiled apple.
A cheap print: not even "sentimental value."

No one bought it at the yard sale.

ii

MEMORY PALACE

Vesalius, scalpel aloft, as he splits like a melon
The hanged man's skull, fragile trepanning to unveil some terra
Incognita of the soul, uncover the seat of memory

Which resides in current, in minute sacs of seawater,
Encoded, shot through with electrical charges.
The cerebral cortex halved, dead wings.

No computer, this, to tell me that today
She's been dead three years, an anniversary marked
Unwittingly by purple tulips in a jar, and seven

Days of April rain. Reliquary. Missed connections. Sentences
Where no one stares from windows longingly. Sentences
Refusing to describe old photographs. Retrievable

And irretrievable, each fragment in its own
Canopic jar. No need to tell me I reside still in that house
Where she's—say it—by the flowerbed, straw hat flaring

And tied with a yellow scarf. *He died of this too,*
She was saying from the couch, where she had to be propped
In a certain way by the nurse, who'd come each morning

With the morphine. *Who?* I said. *Hubert Humphrey.*
He shook hands with me once at the bank. Always smiling.
This borne to the palaces of memory. Loot and booty,

Tribute and ash. The charnel house of memory. Open me,
Observe. The bone saw's snarl. The edifice
Viewed from above, almost an aerial view. Inject

The sinews with purple dye, to circle and arc the synapses
Like footage of squid. Tentacle, ink screen, the dye vats
Of Tyre. *I never did think much of him, but you could see*

The pain on his face every night on the news. He died
You know at home. Doorways, courtyards, bannisters.
Beyond the room, another room. Beyond the room.

WORKMEN PHOTOGRAPHED INSIDE THE REACTOR

—Chernobyl

It passes, you'll remember, through lead. Passes through
the protective suits that don't protect, passes through
every template, roil of hardened magma, each jutting

braincase of Medusan electric wire, each goggle, each mask,
each pike, each sandbag flung by helicopter seven years ago
to cool the meltdown, the pilots soon dead, passes through

the camera of Victoria Ivleva as her flash
picks out the shades in Circle IV, Circle V, Circle VII,
their bone white suits, a single ray of sunlight

slithering through the cracked reactor wall. Two hundred *rems*
per man per month. Passes through the windowpanes
of the empty concrete high rise forty miles away, the single

plastic eye and nylon lashes of a doll on a closet floor. *Each
thought is a rem,* she says, reloading the camera. Each thought
closer to the moment, the spiral more tightly wound:

the communications satellite exhausts its fuel,
the flawless colors of a soccer match in São Paulo
flooded by a gray screen's static hiss, the wreckage

alchemized to shooting stars, smoldering metal
littering Australian deserts. Each thought
coiled more tightly. L. and I beneath the café awning

the morning of the news reports, the Plaza Mayor
in Salamanca, shouted headlines of *El País.*
And all morning the famous courtyard

of the Convent of Las Duenas—the capitals
sprout demons, horned dismembered sandstone heads,
sinners' faces laddering the columns in a double-

helix of damnation, cautionary images
for wealthy nuns of the Golden Age. This one
is eaten by his shriek. This one has become a bleeding tree.

And marble Dante, skullcapped at the fountain,
looking up from the *Comedia*. A cloud,
said the papers, pulsing westward. Each thought, each thought,

the spiral tightening to the plastic tube
lodged in my father's nostrils, *angina pectoris, emphysema,*
his jittery breathing in the next room. The oxygen machine,

umbilical hum and shudder. He has ten days to live.
Point where the circle disappears. The bedroom
I had as a child. Hum and shudder . . . .

I stand with the others as the gate
yawns open, chain link and barbed wire. The white
plastic suits swing from meat hooks in a hallway.

Step in, zip up. The mask, the skullcap,
the rubber gloves reaching up to the elbows,
the pike, the radiometer. Adjust the goggles.

One last breath, last glance at the trees.
Down the staircase to the pit. Each thought—
the pike before me, stabbing at the gloom.

NOTES

"Homage to Ryszard Kapuściński" makes use of material from several of his books, including *The Emperor, The Soccer War,* and *Another Day of Life.*

"Human Form" is for Dean Young.

"Wartime Photos of My Father"; the final section owes a debt to Rilke's "Cadet Portrait of My Father."

"Tomis" is for Belle Waring.

"Emanations"; Daniel Paul Schreber's *Memoirs of My Nervous Illness* (1900) earned him the dubious title of "the most famous schizophrenic in history"; many of Freud's theories regarding schizophrenia were based on his reading of Schreber's book. Schreber's father, the Dr. Spock of his day, was the author of several best-selling guides to child rearing. The device mentioned in the poem was used to train both Daniel Paul and his brother, who later committed suicide.

"Elegy for Empire"; Aspley Cherry-Garrand detailed his experiences as a member of Scott's final polar expedition in an aptly titled memoir, *The Worst Journey in the World.* Cherry-Garrand is known for more than his struggle for the penguin eggs; he also lead the party that discovered the bodies of Scott and his companions. Photographs of Seaman Hartnell's exhumation appear in Owen Beattie and John Geiger's *Frozen in Time;* the deaths of the members of the Franklin expedition were probably hastened by lead poisoning caused by solder in their canned goods.

"The First Six Seals" is for Herbert Morris. Milton Rokeach's *The Three Christs of Ypsilanti* chronicles Dr. Rokeach's work with three schizophrenics, each afflicted with the delusion that he was Christ. By forcing them to live together for a year, Rokeach believed he might be able to cure them. The experiment was not a success.

"Workmen Photographed Inside the Reactor"; the most optimistic estimates of the cleanup time required inside the Chernobyl reactor are about 150 years. The capitals of the inner courtyard of the Convent of Las Duenas in Salamanca are decorated with a profusion of limestone sculptures illustrating scenes from Dante's *Inferno.*

David Wojahn

was born in St. Paul, Minnesota, in 1953, and was educated at the University of Minnesota and the University of Arizona. His first collection, *Icehouse Lights,* was selected by Richard Hugo as the 1981 winner of the Yale Series of Younger Poets competition, and was also chosen as the Poetry Society of America's William Carlos Williams Book Award. His second collection, *Glassworks,* was published by the University of Pittsburgh Press in 1987 and was awarded the Society of Midland Authors' Award for best volume of poetry to be published during that year. *Mystery Train,* his most recent collection, was published by Pittsburgh in 1990. He has received fellowships from the National Endowment for the Arts, the Fine Arts Work Center in Provincetown, and in 1987–88 was the Amy Lowell Traveling Poetry Scholar. He has taught at the University of New Orleans, the University of Arkansas at Little Rock, and the University of Arizona. He currently teaches in the creative writing program at Indiana University and in the MFA in writing program of Vermont College.

PITT POETRY SERIES

ED OCHESTER, GENERAL EDITOR